A Book of PRAYERS for Young Women